···· A **TIMELINE HISTORY** OF THE ····

DECLARATION OF INDEPENDENCE

··**TIMELINE TRACKERS** : AMERICA'S BEGINNINGS ···

ALLAN MOREY

Lerner Publications Company
Minneapolis

CONTENTS

Lerner Publications Company
A division of Lerner Publishing Group, Inc.
241 First Avenue North
Minneapolis, MN 55401 USA

For reading levels and more information, look up this title at www.lernerbooks.com.

Library of Congress Cataloging-in-Publication Data

Morey, Allan.
   A timeline history of the Declaration of Independence / by Allan Morey.
      pages   cm. — (Timeline trackers: America's beginnings)
   Includes index.
   ISBN 978–1–4677–3640–4 (lib. bdg. : alk. paper)
   ISBN 978–1–4677–4752–3 (eBook)
   1. United States. Declaration of Independence—Chronology—Juvenile literature. 2. United States—Politics and government—1775–1783—Chronology—Juvenile literature. I. Title.
E221.M67 2015
973.3'13—dc23   2013043418

Manufactured in the United States of America
1 – BP – 7/15/14

COVER PHOTO:
The five-man drafting committee of the Declaration of
Independence presents their work to Congress.

INTRODUCTION

Starting in the 1500s, Europeans began to colonize North America. By the middle of the 1700s, Great Britain controlled a vast area of thirteen American colonies along the Atlantic Coast of what is now the United States. But over time, tensions grew between Americans and their British rulers. On the one hand, British troops provided protection from French settlers and American Indians who were threatening the colonies' borders. The colonists also had access to Britain's vast trade markets, so they could easily buy and sell supplies. But on the other hand, colonists wanted more control of their lives. They wanted to help make decisions about taxes and laws. Consequently, they wanted their local governments to have more power and to not be subject to the laws of the British Parliament.

But British rulers disagreed. They felt they had the right to run the colonies and to tell the local lawmaking legislatures what to do. After all, Great Britain had helped establish the colonies. It spent a lot of money to keep things running smoothly.

Eventually, the colonists realized that if they wanted a say in government, they would have to declare their independence from Great Britain. That would mean going to war with one of the most powerful countries in the world.

TIMELINES

In this book, a series of dates and important events appear in timelines. Timelines are a graphic way of showing a sequence of events over a specific time period. A timeline often reveals the cause and effect of events. It can help to explain how one happening in history leads to the next. The timelines in this book relay important turning points surrounding the Declaration of Independence. Each timeline is marked with different intervals of time, depending on how close together events happened. In many cases, the interval marks will fall every month or every other month. Solid lines in the timelines indicate regular intervals of time. Dashed lines represent bigger jumps in time.

CHAPTER 1

TROUBLE BREWING

The French and Indian War

From 1754 to 1763, Great Britain and France fought for control of land in the American colonies. In this conflict, known as the French and Indian War, the French army and its American Indian allies fought against the British army and colonial troops. In 1763 the Treaty of Paris ended the war. The treaty

Fireworks in Green Park in London celebrate the signing of the Treaty of Paris in 1763.

May 28, 1754: The first shots of the French and Indian War are fired at the Battle of Jumonville Glen in Pennsylvania.

1762: Chief Pontiac starts to gather support from tribes of the Lake Superior region to fight the new British rulers.

MAY 1754   **SEPT. 1759**   **FEB. 1763**

Sept. 13, 1759: British forces win a big victory over the French at the Battle of Quebec in Canada.

Feb. 10, 1763: The Treaty of Paris brings an end to the French and Indian War with a British victory.

gave Great Britain control of French Canada and all the American lands east of the Mississippi River.

The French and Indian War was just one of many wars that British troops were fighting across the globe. Winning these conflicts was costly, and Great Britain had to borrow money. By the late 1700s, Britain was more than 120 million British pounds in debt, which was an enormous amount of money at the time. The British also were continuing to pay troops to defend the colonies. Many people in Great Britain began to resent having to pay so much to protect land they had never seen.

The Treaty of Paris ended the French and Indian War.

PONTIAC'S WAR

Pontiac was an Ottawa chief in what would become Ohio. He hoped to keep British settlers from moving into areas that the French had once claimed. In spring 1763, he led an attack on a British fort at Detroit and later other British forts in the area. The attacks forced the British Parliament to command British settlers to stay off American Indian lands. While the decision smoothed tensions with American Indians, it angered land-hungry colonial settlers.

July 31, 1763: Chief Pontiac's forces defeat British troops at the Battle of Bloody Run near Richmond, Virginia.

APR. 1763   JUNE 1763   AUG. 1763   OCT. 1763

May 7, 1763: Chief Pontiac leads an attack against the British fort at Detroit.

Oct. 7, 1763: The Royal Proclamation of 1763 bans colonists from settling on American Indian lands west of the Appalachian Mountains.

British Laws

The British Parliament hoped to pay off Britain's war debt through taxes on goods sold to the American colonies. Parliament viewed these taxes as the price the colonies had to pay for British protection and support. The British thought it was only fair to make American colonists pay some of the costs of the war. After all, the fighting had taken place in the colonies. And with the British victory, the colonies had expanded.

The British Parliament passed a series of new tax laws. The first was the Sugar Act of 1764. This law placed higher taxes on sugar and molasses imports into the colonies. It also prevented colonial merchants from buying cheaper goods from countries other than Great Britain. The law also

British ships anchor in the New York Harbor, carrying newly taxed sugar and molasses.

MAR. 1764   MAY 1764   JULY 1764   SEPT. 1764

April 5, 1764: The British Parliament passes the Sugar Act.

Sept. 1, 1764: The British Parliament passes the Currency Act. This law forced colonists to pay debts with British pounds instead of with colonial paper money.

taxed other trade items such as coffee and wine. To pay the taxes, the merchants who traded molasses, coffee, sugar, and wine raised the cost of the goods.

In 1765 the British Parliament passed the Stamp Act. This law affected everyday items. For example, it placed a tax on paper items that nearly every colonist needed. As a result, people had to pay extra for legal documents. Their newspapers cost more, and so did playing cards. Colonists grew angry at the rising costs.

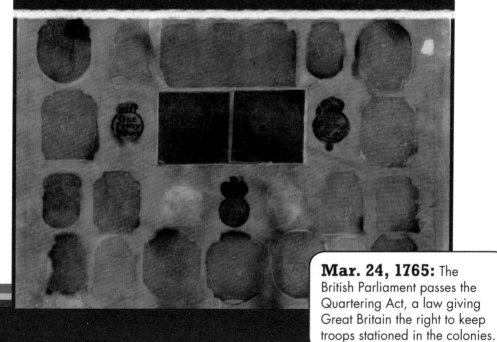

The 1765 Stamp Act created a direct tax of one penny per sheet on newspapers. It required that the newspapers be printed on stamped paper purchased from government agents.

Mar. 24, 1765: The British Parliament passes the Quartering Act, a law giving Great Britain the right to keep troops stationed in the colonies.

Nov. 1764   **Jan. 1765**   **Mar. 1765**   **May 1765**

Mar. 22, 1765: The British Parliament passes the Stamp Act, a tax on all printed-paper items.

May 30, 1765: The lawmakers of the colony of Virginia pass the Virginia Stamp Act Resolutions, speaking out against the Stamp Act.

The Sons of Liberty

The Stamp Act angered colonists. They did not like paying higher prices for everyday items. And they did not like that Great Britain was raising money by taxing the colonies. The colonists also had no say in how the tax money was spent. Instead, Parliament decided how to spend it. Colonists called this taxation without representation.

A group of shopkeepers in Boston were fiercely opposed to the law. Known as the Sons of Liberty, they organized protests

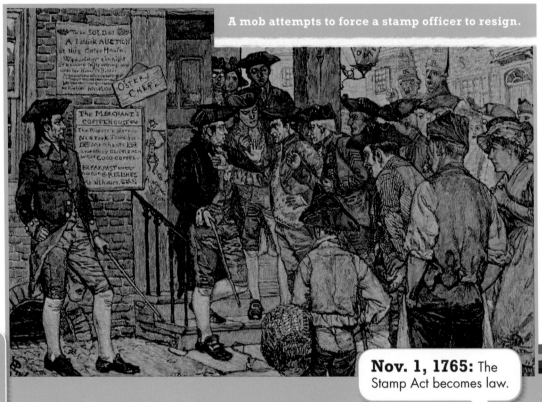

A mob attempts to force a stamp officer to resign.

Nov. 1, 1765: The Stamp Act becomes law.

Aug. 1765   **Sept. 1765**   **Oct. 1765**   **Nov. 1765**

Aug. 14, 1765: The Sons of Liberty protest the Stamp Act by burning a likeness of Andrew Oliver.

Oct. 7, 1765: Representatives of nine colonies first gather for the Stamp Act Congress. At this meeting, they make a list of complaints and ask the British government to repeal certain unpopular laws.

against the Stamp Act. On the night of August 14, 1765, they hung a likeness of Andrew Oliver from a tree and burned it. Oliver was a wealthy merchant and government official. His job was to collect the stamp tax fees. Later that night, protesters threw stones at Oliver's house. The crowd was so large that British officials could not control it.

Soon, Sons of Liberty groups were popping up in every colony. They pressured British officials in charge of collecting taxes to quit. The pressure was so great that Parliament repealed the Stamp Act in 1766.

The Sons of Liberty gather under the Liberty Tree in Boston.

DEC. 1765　JAN. 1766　FEB. 1766　MAR. 1766

Mar. 18, 1766: The British Parliament repeals the Stamp Act and passes the Declaratory Act. The Declaratory Act states that only Parliament can pass laws affecting the colonies.

The Townshend Acts

The British Parliament looked for new ways to raise taxes. In 1767 Parliament passed the Townshend Acts, which forced merchants to pay taxes on imported items such as paint, lead, glass, and tea shipped from Great Britain to the colonies. The merchants raised prices on the goods, passing along the extra costs to buyers. As tensions and anger grew in the colonies, Great Britain began sending more soldiers to keep peace. They were also there to enforce payment of the new taxes.

Many colonists were angry that Britain expected the colonies to pay for the troops. They also thought the new taxes were unfair. They felt that Great Britain did not have the right to tax them because the colonists were not represented in Parliament. In

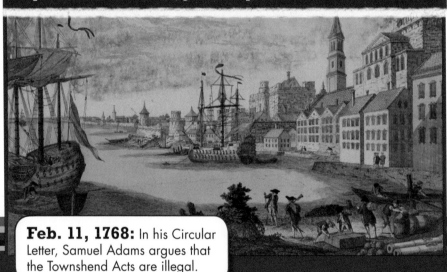

Two British ships are anchored in the Boston Harbor, carrying imported items such as tea, glass, and paint.

Feb. 11, 1768: In his Circular Letter, Samuel Adams argues that the Townshend Acts are illegal.

JUNE 1767   **FEB. 1768**   **APR. 1768**   **JUNE 1768**

June 15, 1767: The British Parliament begins passing a series of laws known together as the Townshend Acts.

Apr. 5, 1768: Merchants in New York City form the colonies' first Chamber of Commerce. Many of its leaders supported colonial independence.

protest, many colonists boycotted British goods. If they didn't buy items from Great Britain, they would not have to pay the taxes.

With the boycott, British imports to the colonies decreased by nearly half. British merchants and the British economy lost so much money that Parliament repealed most of the Townshend Acts. The British left only the tax on tea in place.

Samuel Adams

CIRCULAR LETTER

Samuel Adams, who was elected to the Massachusetts legislature in 1765, was one of the most outspoken American patriots. While many colonists asked for representation in the British Parliament, Adams thought this was not possible. Great Britain was on the other side of the Atlantic Ocean. It would be too difficult for American colonists to attend parliamentary meetings. Instead, he argued that each colony's own governing body should have control over local taxes and laws. In February 1768, he wrote a letter in which he claimed that the Townshend Acts were illegal. The letter began circulating, or moving, throughout the colonies. For that reason, it became known as the Circular Letter.

Oct. 1, 1768: Additional British troops begin arriving in Boston to maintain order.

AUG. 1768   **OCT. 1768**   **DEC. 1768**   **MAY 1769**

Aug. 1, 1768: Merchants in Boston agree to the Boston Non-Importation Agreement, vowing not to trade with Great Britain.

May 16, 1769: With the Virginia Resolves of 1769, Virginia's legislature claims that the Townshend Acts are illegal.

CHAPTER 2

ACTS of DEFIANCE

The Boston Massacre

On a cold spring day in 1770, a group of colonists gathered outside the Custom House, where colonists in Boston paid their taxes. The colonists were shouting at a British soldier standing guard. British captain Thomas Preston led several soldiers to aid the guard. More colonists gathered, and soon they were throwing rocks and snowballs at the soldiers.

Suddenly, several shots were fired. Historians are not sure if Captain Preston gave

The Boston Massacre of 1770 left five American patriots dead at the hands of a group of British soldiers.

Mar. 5, 1770: In the Boston Massacre, British soldiers fire upon a group of colonists, killing five.

MAR. 1770   **MAY 1770**   **JULY 1770**

Apr. 12, 1770: The British Parliament repeals all the Townshend taxes, except for the one on tea.

BOSTON MASSACRE

the order to fire or if a soldier fired his musket accidentally. When the smoke cleared, however, five colonists were dead. Several others were injured. Captain Preston and his men were arrested and charged with murder. The event came to be known as the Boston Massacre.

JOHN ADAMS

Boston lawyer John Adams was one of the Founding Fathers of the United States, and he would go on to become the nation's second president in 1797. But before that he was very unpopular. When the colonial government accused Captain Thomas Preston and his soldiers of murder, Adams agreed to defend them. Even though he opposed British rule, he thought it was important to give the soldiers a fair trial.

At the trial, Adams argued that the soldiers acted in self-defense. Preston and all but two of the soldiers involved in the Boston Massacre were found innocent.

Nov. 27, 1770: The trials of the soldiers under Captain Preston's command begin.

SEPT. 1770   NOV. 1770   JAN. 1771

Oct. 24, 1770: Captain Thomas Preston's trial begins.

Dec. 5, 1770: The trials of the soldiers under Captain Preston's command end. Two are found guilty of manslaughter.

The Committees of Correspondence

In the 1700s, the colonies had few roads and limited communication to connect them. Also, life in one colony was often very different from life in another colony. Even though the colonies were all ruled by Britain, they did not see themselves as one unified community. However, conflict with Great Britain began to change that. People throughout the colonies were angered by British taxes and laws.

As a way to work together against the British, colonists in Boston set up a Committee of Correspondence

A Committee of Correspondence decides how to respond to a letter from Boston describing British plans to punish the city for the Boston Tea Party.

June 10, 1772: Angry colonists set fire to the *Gaspée* after wounding its captain and capturing the crew.

APR. 1772   JUNE 1772   AUG. 1772

June 9, 1772: The HMS *Gaspée*, a British naval ship that was patrolling for merchant ships engaged in illegal trade, runs aground off the coast of Rhode Island.

in 1772. The group's goal was to argue for colonists' rights. It would also work to improve communications with the other colonies. In 1773 Virginia's legislature recommended that each colony set up its own Committee of Correspondence. With better communication, the colonies could be more united in their struggle against the British.

American patriots burn the British customs ship *Gaspée* on June 9, 1772.

Nov. 2, 1772: Colonists in Boston form the first Committee of Correspondence to organize resistance to the British.

Mar. 12, 1773: Virginia's legislature recommends that each colony set up a Committee of Correspondence.

Oct. 1772   Dec. 1772   Feb. 1773   Apr. 1773

Nov. 20, 1772: Boston's Committee of Correspondence circulates the Boston Pamphlet, a letter discussing colonial rights.

Mar. 26, 1773: North Carolina sets up a Committee of Correspondence.

The Tea Act

American colonists were angry about British taxes. But they also did not like the limits Great Britain placed on trade with the colonies. For example, Britain declared that most goods shipped to the colonies had to come from British markets.

In 1773 Parliament passed the Tea Act. At first, colonists thought this law was a good thing. It lowered the tax on tea, which most colonists drank. But it only lowered the tax on tea coming from Britain's East India Company. Tea coming from Dutch traders was taxed at a higher rate.

Colonists were angry that Britain was limiting trade and controlling pricing in this way. So they boycotted tea from the East India Company. When several British ships with cargos of tea docked in Boston

BOSTON TEA PARTY

The Boston Tea Party is probably one of the Sons of Liberty's most famous acts. In December 1773, Samuel Adams organized a group of sixty colonists. They disguised themselves as Mohawk American Indians. Then late at night, they boarded the *Dartmouth*, the *Eleanor*, and the *Beaver*. These East India Company ships were docked in Boston Harbor. The raiding party quickly broke into the ships' holds. They brought the crates of tea on deck and dumped their contents into the harbor.

Apr. 27, 1773: The British Parliament passes the Tea Act.

APR. 1773

JUNE 1773

AUG. 1773

May 10, 1773: The Tea Act goes into effect.

Harbor, colonial officials asked them to leave. British royal governor Thomas Hutchinson refused to send the ships away. So the Sons of Liberty took action. They dumped the tea into the harbor.

Oct. 1773: Delaware sets up a Committee of Correspondence.

Dec. 2, 1773: The HMS *Eleanor* arrives in Boston.

Dec. 15, 1773: The HMS *Beaver* arrives in Boston.

OCT. 1773

DEC. 1773

FEB. 1774

Nov. 28, 1773: The HMS *Dartmouth* arrives in Boston.

Dec. 16, 1773: The Sons of Liberty organize a raid on British East India Company tea ships, dumping tea into Boston Harbor in an event known as the Boston Tea Party.

The Coercive Acts

Even though they wore disguises, the Boston Tea Party participants were widely known. The British Parliament was angry. Members knew that the Sons of Liberty were responsible for the raid. In response, Parliament passed a series of laws known as the Coercive Acts. These laws were meant to stop further resistance to British rule.

One part of the Coercive Acts was the British Port Bill. This law closed the Boston port until the residents of Boston paid for damages from the Boston Tea Party. The Massachusetts Government Act put a military government in place in the colony. It also outlawed colonists

> This document outlines the British plan to close Boston's port after colonists rebelled by throwing tea in the Boston Harbor.

Act for blocking up the Harbour of *Boston*.

May 12, 1774: Angered by the Boston Port Bill, merchants in Boston vote to renew the Boston Non-Importation Agreement.

APR. 1, 1774   APR. 15, 1774   MAY 1, 1774   MAY 15, 1774

Mar. 31, 1774: The British Parliament passes the Boston Port Bill.

May 13, 1774: Great Britain sends four regiments of soldiers to Boston to maintain order.

from holding town meetings. The Administration of Justice Act prevented British officials from being tried for crimes in the colonies. The new Quartering Act required colonists to house British troops in their own homes if requested. Previously, they had only been required to provide soldiers with some sort of shelter.

The colonists were outraged by these laws, all part of the Coercive Acts. They called them the Intolerable Acts.

British troops occupy Boston.

June 2, 1774: The British Parliament passes the new Quartering Act.

JUNE 1, 1774   JUNE 15, 1774   JULY 1, 1774   JULY 15, 1774

May 20, 1774: The British Parliament passes the Massachusetts Government Act and the Administration of Justice Act. Pennsylvania sets up a Committee of Correspondence.

July 1774: Virginia lawyer and lawmaker Thomas Jefferson writes "A Summary View of the Rights of British America," an article arguing that Great Britain did not have the right to govern the thirteen colonies.

The First Continental Congress

In response to the Coercive Acts, leaders from across the colonies decided to come together. Small acts of protest were not enough to challenge the British, so colonial leaders asked each colony to send delegates to a meeting in Philadelphia.

Delegates met at the First Continental Congress in September 1774. The meeting was a first step toward creating a government that would represent all the colonies.

In all, fifty people from twelve of the thirteen colonies met at Philadelphia's Carpenters' Hall. Founding Fathers

The First Continental Congress met at Carpenters' Hall in Philadelphia, Pennsylvania, in 1774.

Sept. 17, 1774: The First Continental Congress declares its opposition to the Coercive Acts.

AUG. 15, 1774   **SEPT. 1, 1774**   **SEPT. 15, 1774**

Sept. 5, 1774: Delegates from twelve of the thirteen colonies form the First Continental Congress.

George Washington (a lawmaker from Virginia), Samuel Adams (from Boston), and Patrick Henry (a lawyer and lawmaker from Virginia) were among them.

At the meeting, members issued a declaration of colonial rights. This declaration was a list of grievances against the British government. These included unfair taxes and not having representation in Parliament. The group pledged to boycott British goods until these complaints were addressed. The Congress's goal was not independence but to gain fair treatment.

This letter urged Americans not to purchase goods from Great Britain.

BOSTON, June 10, 1774.

GENTLEMEN,

WHEREAS several of our brethren, members of the committees of correspondence in the neighbouring towns, have since our letter of the 8th instant applied to us, to know whether it was expected that the form of the covenant which we inclosed in our letter should be literally adopted by the several towns : We have thought it necessary to inform our respectable fellow countrymen, that the committee, neither in this or any other matter mean to dictate to them, but are humbly of opinion, that if they keep to the spirit of that covenant, and solemnly engage not to purchase any goods which shall be imported from Great Britain after the time stipulated, and agree to suspend dealing with such persons as shall persist in counteracting the salutary design, by continuing to import or purchase British articles so imported, the end we proposed will be fully answered, and the salvation of North-America, under providence, thereby insured.

We are,

Gentlemen,

Your friends and fellow countrymen,

Signed by order and in behalf of the committee of Correspondence for Boston.

William Cooper Clerk

Oct. 7, 1774: The Massachusetts Provincial Congress forms to help towns in the colony communicate.

Oct. 20, 1774: In the Articles of Association, members of the Continental Congress vow not to trade with Great Britain.

OCT. 1, 1774   OCT. 15, 1774   NOV. 1, 1774

Oct. 14, 1774: In a declaration of colonial rights, delegates at the First Continental Congress list their grievances against the British government.

Oct. 26, 1774: The First Continental Congress adjourns.

CHAPTER 3

THE BRITISH ARE COMING!

Give Me Liberty or Give Me Death!

King George III of Great Britain refused to negotiate with the American colonists. The British felt the colonies had a duty to remain loyal to Great Britain no matter what.

Colonists such as Patrick Henry did not agree. While some colonists wished to settle things peacefully with Great Britain, Henry was more radical. He worried that at some point, the British might respond

King George III

Feb. 1, 1775: Colonists in Massachusetts begin collecting weapons in preparation for war with the British.

FEB. 1, 1775   FEB. 15, 1775   MAR. 1, 1775

Feb. 9, 1775: The British Parliament passes a resolution declaring that the colonies are in a state of rebellion.

to the colonists with military action. Henry wanted to create a militia (citizen army) to defend Virginia. He wanted to meet the British with force.

In March 1775, at a meeting of Virginia's legislature, Henry gave a famous speech in support of self-rule for the colonies. He talked about the long struggle to work with Great Britain for greater freedom and fair treatment. He argued that peaceful measures were not working. It was time to stand up and fight. He ended his speech with the famous words "Give me liberty or give me death!"

Patrick Henry delivers an impassioned speech at a 1775 meeting of Virginia's legislature.

Mar. 23, 1775: Patrick Henry gives his famous "Give me liberty or give me death!" speech at a meeting of the Virginia legislature.

Mar. 30, 1775: The British Parliament passes the New England Restraining Act, requiring New England colonies to trade only with Great Britain.

Mar. 15, 1775

Apr. 1, 1775

Apr. 15, 1775

Mar. 28, 1775: Explorers led by Daniel Boone begin a trek across the Appalachian Mountains to settle Kentucky as the fourteenth colony.

Battles of Lexington and Concord

The British knew that the colonists were arming themselves. They had heard rumors of a stash of weapons hidden near Concord, Massachusetts.

British general Thomas Gage had orders to take the colonists' weapons. He was also charged with capturing John Hancock (president of the First Continental Congress) and Samuel Adams. Gage's plans were to have British

The Battle of Lexington was the first military engagement of the American Revolutionary War.

APR. 16, 1775

APR. 17, 1775

APR. 18, 1775

Apr. 16, 1775: Paul Revere tells patriots at Concord, Massachusetts, to move weapons stored there.

Apr. 18, 1775: British troops approach Concord. Paul Revere, William Dawes, and Samuel Prescott ride to warn the patriots.

soldiers march to Lexington, Massachusetts, where Adams and Hancock were staying. Gage's troops would then go to Concord and seize the weapons.

At Lexington a small group of colonial troops met the British forces. The first shots of the Revolutionary War rang out. Outnumbered, the colonists quickly retreated. The British then continued their march to Concord. But more and more militiamen were gathering. They prevented the British from reaching Concord. As the British retreated to Boston, militiamen fired at them from behind trees and fence posts. The battles were quick and bloody, leaving 273 British casualties and 95 American casualties.

THE RIDE OF PAUL REVERE

Paul Revere was a Massachusetts silversmith who supported the patriot cause. He was among several horseback riders who carried messages back and forth between revolutionaries. Revere rode to Concord on April 16, 1775, to warn his fellow patriots to move their weapon stores. Two days later, he found out British troops were on the move. He and another patriot messenger, William Dawes, each rode separately to warn the colonial troops at Lexington. When British patrols stopped both men, another rider, Samuel Prescott, rode ahead to give the warning at Concord. Because of their efforts, patriot troops were ready for the British. Revere's heroism was made famous by Henry Wadsworth Longfellow's poem "Paul Revere's Ride," published in 1863.

APR. 19, 1775

APR. 20, 1775

APR. 21, 1775

Apr. 19, 1775: The first shots of the Revolutionary War are fired at the Battles of Lexington and Concord. The Siege of Boston begins.

The Second Continental Congress

The American colonists knew they needed to meet again. This time, they would prepare for war with Great Britain. Delegates from all thirteen colonies met in Philadelphia for the Second Continental Congress.

One of the first orders of business was to establish an army. The Continental Congress gave command of this army

Members of the Second Continental Congress gather in the Assembly Room of the Pennsylvania State House in Philadelphia, Pennsylvania.

May 10, 1775:
Colonial delegates meet in Philadelphia for the Second Continental Congress.

MAY 1, 1775   MAY 15, 1775   JUNE 1, 1775

May 1775: Delegates to the Second Continental Congress debate whether the colonies should fight for independence.

May 10, 1775: Colonial forces capture Fort Ticonderoga in New York, taking important artillery from the British.

to George Washington, a delegate from Virginia. He had also served as a commander during the French and Indian War.

Many colonial delegates did not want to go to war. Great Britain was one of the most powerful countries in the world. Some of the delegates worried it would not be possible to win a war against such a mighty enemy. Many had also come from Great Britain. They felt loyal to their homeland.

George Washington

These colonists hoped the conflict could be resolved peacefully, without bloodshed. One such colonist and delegate was John Dickinson from Delaware. He wrote the Olive Branch Petition. In it, he spoke out against British laws but said that the colonies would remain loyal to Great Britain if they were treated fairly.

June 15, 1775: The Congress appoints George Washington commander in chief of the Continental Army.

July 6, 1775: The Congress issues the Declaration of the Causes and Necessity of Taking Up Arms, urging the king to restore the rights of the colonies to end the conflict swiftly.

JUNE 15, 1775   JULY 1, 1775   JULY 15, 1775

June 14, 1775: The Second Continental Congress establishes a Continental Army.

July 5, 1775: Hoping to avoid an all-out war, the Second Continental Congress issues the Olive Branch Petition.

July 8, 1775: The Congress sends the Olive Branch Petition to King George III.

The Battle of Bunker Hill

Boston Harbor had always been an important colonial trading port. It was also a hotbed of resistance to British rule. Many British soldiers were stationed there. As fighting broke out in 1775, these British troops took control of the city.

Several hills lay outside the city. Colonial forces knew that

This oil painting depicts the death of General Joseph Warren at the Battle of Bunker Hill.

June 16, 1775: Colonel William Prescott leads an army of twelve hundred soldiers to Breed's Hill, hoping to gain control of the area before the British do.

JUNE 10, 1775   JUNE 15, 1775   JUNE 20, 1775

June 15, 1775: The American colonists receive word that British troops in Boston are planning to take control of the Charlestown Peninsula, where Bunker Hill and Breed's Hill are located.

June 17, 1775: The first major battle of the Revolutionary War, known as the Battle of Bunker Hill, takes place on Breed's Hill outside of Boston.

if they could control those hills, they could bombard the city and possibly force the British troops to retreat. On the night of June 16, 1775, colonial troops marched across the Charlestown Peninsula, north of Boston. They climbed to the top of Breed's Hill and dug in. The next day, British forces were surprised to see colonial soldiers staring down at them from across the Mystic River.

Major General William Howe ordered his redcoat troops to storm the hill. The colonial forces drove them back again and again. Eventually, the colonial soldiers ran low on ammunition. They turned to hand-to-hand combat with bayonets. Outnumbered, they were forced to retreat.

The battle was a costly victory for the British. More than one thousand British soldiers were either wounded or killed. The Continental Army suffered less than half as many casualties.

BATTLE OF WHERE?

The Battle of Bunker Hill did not actually take place on Bunker Hill. Colonel William Prescott had orders to fortify Bunker Hill, but he and his troops ended up on Breed's Hill instead. Historians are not sure exactly how this happened. The troops could have lost their way in the darkness of night or used a mislabeled map. Or Prescott may have chosen the hill that was closer to the Mystic River because he thought it was a stronger position for attacking the British.

JUNE 25, 1775

JULY 1, 1775

JULY 5, 1775

June 22, 1775: The Second Continental Congress decides to print money to pay for a war against Great Britain.

July 3, 1775: George Washington takes command of the Continental Army in Cambridge, Massachusetts.

CHAPTER 4

The CALL for INDEPENDENCE

Common Sense and Early Rebellions

The voices calling for American independence were growing louder and louder. Along with Samuel Adams and Patrick

Thomas Paine

Henry, writer Thomas Paine, who had recently arrived in Pennsylvania from Great Britain, strongly believed in independence. In January 1776, he anonymously published a pamphlet titled *Common Sense*.

In *Common Sense*, Paine wrote about the evils of Britain's constitutional monarchy. In this type of government, a parliament passes laws that a king or a queen enforces. But a

Dec. 22, 1775: The British Parliament passes the Prohibitory Act, blocking American ports and halting trade with the colonies.

OCT. 1775	NOV. 1775	DEC. 1775	JAN. 1776

Oct. 27, 1775: In the Royal Proclamation of Rebellion, King George III urges Parliament to act quickly to end the colonies' rebellion.

Jan. 10, 1776: Thomas Paine publishes *Common Sense*.

king or a queen usually has limitless power and can abuse that power. Paine went on to say that independence was the only way the colonies could prosper.

Half a million copies of *Common Sense* were printed. People throughout the colonies read the pamphlet. Most political leaders were already leaning toward declaring independence. Many historians credit Paine's writings for convincing average citizens as well.

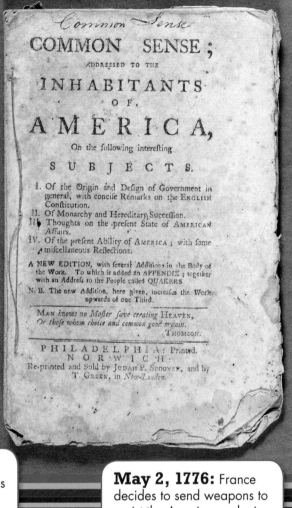

Thomas Paine began writing his famous forty-eight-page pamphlet in 1775, which was originally titled *Plain Truth*.

Mar. 4, 1776: The Continental Army captures Dorchester Heights, overlooking Boston.

May 2, 1776: France decides to send weapons to assist the American colonies.

FEB. 1776   MAR. 1776   APR. 1776   MAY 1776

May 4, 1776: Rhode Island becomes the first colony to formally declare independence from Great Britain.

The Declaration of Independence

In May 1776, the Second Continental Congress met once again. By this time, several battles had been fought. The demands for independence were deafening.

Richard Henry Lee, a delegate from Virginia, led the cry for independence. Yet some delegates argued that it was too soon. They felt that additional steps, such as forming a central government, should be taken before declaring independence.

Richard Henry Lee

Others argued that independence was necessary. Great Britain was already waging war on the colonies. And it was the only way to end unfair taxes and British control of trade.

In the end, the Congress voted to set up a committee

June 7, 1776: Delegate Richard Henry Lee, who served in the Virginia legislature, proposes to the Continental Congress that the colonies should be independent states.

Apr. 1776: North Carolina becomes the first colony to empower its delegates to vote for independence.

APR. 1, 1776   MAY 1, 1776   JUNE 7, 1776   JUNE 8, 1776

May 15, 1776: Virginia tells its delegates at the Second Continental Congress to ask for a declaration of independence.

June 8, 1776: Debate over whether to declare independence begins.

to write a formal declaration of independence. Thomas Jefferson, John Adams, Benjamin Franklin of Philadelphia, Roger Sherman of Connecticut, and Robert R. Livingston of New York were appointed to this group. They gave Jefferson the job of writing the first draft.

The Second Continental Congress delegated (*from left to right*) Thomas Jefferson, Roger Sherman, Benjamin Franklin, Robert R. Livingston, and John Adams to write the Declaration of Independence.

June 11, 1776: The Continental Congress sets up a committee to draft a declaration of independence.

JUNE 9, 1776   JUNE 10, 1776   JUNE 11, 1776   JUNE 12, 1776

June 12, 1776: Virginia passes its own Declaration of Rights, a document that inspired the first few paragraphs of the Declaration of Independence.

Thomas Jefferson and Approval of the Declaration

Thomas Jefferson kept the Declaration of Independence short and to the point. His main point was that people have rights and freedoms that a government cannot ignore. When it does, the people have the right to separate from an oppressive government. He wrote that all people have the

Thomas Jefferson

right to "Life, Liberty and the pursuit of Happiness."

Jefferson also spelled out some of the grievances the colonies had with King George III's rule. The declaration stated that King George did not allow colonies to make laws that were necessary and that Britain had cut off the colonies' trade with other countries. In effect, Britain had taken all power away from colonial governments.

Some heated debate followed Jefferson's presentation of the

July 2, 1776: Delegates from twelve colonies vote in favor of declaring independence.

JUNE 25, 1776

JULY 1, 1776

JULY 5, 1776

June 28, 1776: Thomas Jefferson presents the Declaration of Independence to the Second Continental Congress.

July 4, 1776: The Continental Congress formally adopts Thomas Jefferson's Declaration of Independence.

Declaration of Independence to the Congress. In his original draft, Jefferson had criticized King George for allowing slavery in the colonies. But delegates from southern colonies, where slavery was common, would not sign a document that opposed slavery. So the passage was cut.

On July 2, 1776, the delegates of twelve colonies voted unanimously in favor of the declaration. Several days later, the delegates of New York voted in favor as well. From then on, the United States of America considered itself an independent nation.

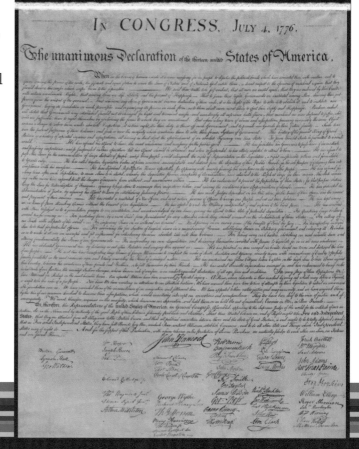

The Declaration of Independence officially announced that the thirteen American colonies were seceding from Great Britain.

JULY 10, 1776

JULY 15, 1776

AUG. 5, 1776

July 12, 1776: The first draft of the Articles of Confederation, which would later become the first US constitution, is presented to the Continental Congress.

Aug. 2, 1776: The delegates of the Second Continental Congress sign the Declaration of Independence.

Fight for Independence

Declaring independence was one thing. Winning freedom was another. The colonial army hoped to hold off the superior British army just long enough for another country to come to the aid of the Americans.

Early in 1776, British troops left Boston. They set their sights on New York City. General George Washington quickly moved his forces to protect the city. The two armies met in late

George Washington crossed the Delaware River on Christmas Day in 1776 in order to surprise British troops in Trenton, New Jersey.

AUG. 1776

SEPT. 1776

OCT. 1776

Aug. 27, 1776: British forces win the Battle of Long Island in New York.

Oct. 26, 1776: Benjamin Franklin sets sail for France to seek military and financial support for fighting the British.

August on Long Island. Washington's men were outnumbered and barely escaped capture.

The British attacked the Continental Army again at White Plains, New York. Washington was forced to retreat once more. Then with a victory at the Battle of Fort Washington, the British took control of New York City. The Continental Army was forced to retreat through New Jersey and into Philadelphia.

After these defeats, Washington's men were demoralized. Many deserted. Washington himself worried that the war—and American independence—might be lost.

CROSSING THE DELAWARE

During the winter of 1776, George Washington thought the war was nearly lost. He knew a daring move was needed. On Christmas Day, he ordered his forces to cross the icy Delaware River from New York back into New Jersey. Under cover of night, he and his men surprised British forces at Trenton and scored an easy victory. Washington quickly followed up by defeating the British at the Battle of Princeton. While the war was far from finished, winning these two battles helped the colonists believe that the war could be won.

Nov. 16, 1776: After a victory at the Battle of Fort Washington, British forces take control of New York City.

Dec. 25, 1776: George Washington begins his crossing of the Delaware River.

NOV. 1776   DEC. 1776   JAN. 1777

Oct. 28, 1776: British forces win the Battle of White Plains.

Dec. 26, 1776: The Continental Army defeats British forces at the Battle of Trenton in New Jersey.

France to the Rescue

Early in the Revolutionary War, the Continental Army suffered defeat after defeat. Other countries believed that the colonists might not be able to win their independence. France, Spain, and the Netherlands were willing to lend the United States money and send weapons. But they would not send troops.

Until the colonies had formally declared their independence, other European countries were not willing to interfere. They felt that Britain had a right to rule its colonies as it saw fit. Once the colonies had formally declared their independence, other nations began to send money and troops.

The Continental Army scored an impressive victory at the Battle of Saratoga in 1777. This gave France

The British Army concedes to the Continental Army at the Battle of Saratoga in 1777.

Jan. 3, 1777: The Continental Army defeats British forces at the Battle of Princeton in New Jersey.

Nov. 15, 1777: The Continental Congress approves the Articles of Confederation.

1776

1777

1778

Oct. 17, 1777: The Continental Army wins a decisive victory at the Battle of Saratoga, turning the tide of the war.

Feb. 6, 1778: France and the United States sign the Treaty of Alliance.

confidence that the colonists could win their freedom from Great Britain. The French were then more than willing to aid in a war against an old rival.

In February 1778, France and the colonies signed the Treaty of Alliance. Shortly afterward, Great Britain declared war on France. French soldiers were soon on their way to support the colonists' cause.

France's first minister to America, Conrad Alexandre Gérard, meets members of the Second Continental Congress following the signing of the Treaty of Alliance in 1778.

Mar. 29, 1780: The Siege of Charleston begins in South Carolina as British forces hope to capture one of the most important southern cities in the United States.

1779

1780

1781

May 12, 1780: Continental forces defending Charleston surrender to the British.

Conclusion

In 1781, after six years of fighting, the British army found itself surrounded at Yorktown, Virginia. After three weeks of fighting, British general Charles Cornwallis realized he had no choice but to surrender.

Peace negotiations began the following spring. John Adams, Benjamin Franklin, and American diplomat John Jay represented the United States during the talks. The Treaty of Paris, signed in 1783, ended the war. The United States was officially recognized as an independent nation, equal in status to Great Britain, its former colonizer, and to the other powerful European nations.

The Declaration of Independence was and remains an important symbol of freedom. It set the stage for the American fight for independence. And through its ideas that all people are created equal and have certain rights that cannot be

The United States and Great Britain meet in Paris to sign a treaty in 1783.

CONCLUSION

Jan. 17, 1781: With a victory at the Battle of Cowpens, in South Carolina, the Continental Army takes control of the South.

Oct. 7, 1780: At the Battle of Kings Mountain, in South Carolina, patriots defeat loyalists supporting the British, helping to turn the tide in the colonies' favor.

Mar. 1, 1781: The colonies ratify the Articles of Confederation, establishing a federal government.

Nov. 1780   Jan. 1781   Mar. 1781   May 1781   July 1781

taken away, the declaration inspired other freedom movements around the world. For example, in the late 1780s, French revolutionaries launched a fight for freedom from monarchic rule in their country, shortly after Americans won their freedom. And Americans looking for freedom from oppression have looked to the declaration for inspiration over the decades. Every July 4, Americans mark the signing of the Declaration of Independence as Independence Day. It is a celebration of what freedom means to all Americans.

People can see the original Declaration of Independence at the National Archives in Washington, DC.

Sept. 3, 1783: Delegates sign the Treaty of Paris, officially ending the American Revolution.

Sept. 28, 1781: The Siege of Yorktown begins.

SEPT. 1781   NOV. 1781   SEPT. 1783   JUNE 1870

Oct. 19, 1781: British general Cornwallis signs the Articles of Capitulation, signaling the end of fighting.

June 28, 1870: Congress votes for the first time to make July 4 an official holiday for federal employees.

Writing Activity

From Thomas Paine's *Common Sense* to Samuel Adams's Circular Letter, Americans voiced their opinions through writing. At the time, people did not have televisions, radios, or computers to spread information and share opinions. Instead, they passed around printed letters or they published pamphlets for sale. The goal was to persuade people to support an idea.

Imagine you are living in America at the time of the struggle for independence. How would you feel about the British tax laws or British control of international trade? Pick one of the laws you have read about and write down your arguments for or against the act. From the point of view of a patriot, how would the law affect you, your family, and your friends? Would the law force you to do something you would not want to do?

What would you think if you were a loyalist to British rule? How might you convince people that the act is fair? What would you say to make people believe that the law did not cause harm?

June 2, 1774: The British Parliament passes the new Quartering Act.

March 22, 1765: The British Parliament passes the Stamp Act, a tax on all printed-paper items.

April 27, 1773: The British Parliament passes the Tea Act.

March 24, 1765: The British Parliament passes the Quartering Act, a law giving Great Britain the right to keep troops stationed in the colonies.

April 5, 1764: The British Parliament passes the Sugar Act.

Sept. 1, 1764: The British Parliament passes the Currency Act. This law forced colonists to pay debts with British pounds instead of with colonial paper money.

June 15, 1767: The British Parliament begins passing a series of laws known together as the Townshend Acts.

May 20, 1774: The British Parliament passes the Massachusetts Government Act and the Administration of Justice Act. Pennsylvania sets up a Committee of Correspondence.

March 31, 1774: The British Parliament passes the Boston Port Bill.

Source Notes

25 "Patrick Henry," *Encyclopædia Britannica*, accessed December 11, 2013, http://www.britannica.com/EBchecked/topic/261398/Patrick-Henry.

36 "The Declaration of Independence: A Transcription," *The Charters of Freedom*, National Archives, accessed December 5, 2013, http://www.archives.gov/exhibits/charters/declaration_transcript.html.

Glossary

boycott: to refuse to buy goods from an organization or country

delegate: someone who represents the interests of a group at a meeting

loyalist: an American colonist who was loyal to Great Britain

militia: an emergency military force made up of civilians who are not part of a regular army

patriot: an American colonist who supported fighting for independence from Great Britain

radical: having extreme political views

ratify: to approve something such as a law or declaration, usually by voting for or signing a document

redcoat: a British soldier, known for the color of the army uniform

repeal: to reverse a law, usually through a vote

treaty: a written agreement between two or more parties to define the terms of a surrender or of trade agreements

Further Information

The American Revolution
http://www.theamericanrevolution.org
Visit this site for information about the battles, the people, and the events of the American Revolution.

Kostyal, K. M. *Founding Fathers: The Fight for Freedom and the Birth of America.* Washington, DC: National Geographic Books, 2014. This book explores the United States' fight for freedom.

Micklos, John, Jr. *The Making of the United States from Thirteen Colonies—through Primary Sources.* Berkeley Heights, NJ: Enslow Publishers, 2013. Through primary sources, this book examines the early history of the United States.

Our Documents
http://www.ourdocuments.gov/index.php?flash=true&
Visit this site to see copies of famous documents, from the Declaration of Independence to the US Constitution.

Ransom, Candice. *What Was the Continental Congress? And Other Questions about the Declaration of Independence.* Minneapolis: Lerner Publications, 2011. This book answers many questions about the colonies' fight for independence.

Santella, Andrew. *The French and Indian War.* New York: Children's Press, 2012. Read this book to learn more about the French and Indian War.

US Department of State, Office of the Historian, Milestones: 1750–1775
http://history.state.gov/milestones/1750-1775
This site covers important events leading up to the signing of the Declaration of Independence.

LERNER
SOURCE

Expand learning beyond the printed book. Download free, complementary educational resources for this book from our website, www.lerneresource.com.

Index

Photo Acknowledgments

The images in this book are used with the permission of: © Bibliotheque Nationale, Paris, France/The Bridgeman Art Library, pp. 4–5; © Gerald Coke Handel Collection, Foundling Museum, London/The Bridgeman Art Library, p. 6; © Archives du Ministere des Affaires Etrangeres, Paris, France/The Bridgeman Art Library, p. 7; © Private Collection/Peter Newark Pictures/The Bridgeman Art Library, pp. 8, 11, 21, 35; © Massachusetts Historical Society, Boston, MA, USA/The Bridgeman Art Library, p. 9; © The Mob Attempting to Force a Stamp Officer to Resign, from Harper's Magazine, 1882 (litho), Pyle, Howard (1853-1911) (after)/Private Collection/The Bridgeman Art Library, p. 10; Library of Congress LC-DIG-ppmsca-30573, p. 12; Courtesy Everett Collection, p. 13; Library of Congress LC-USZC4-4600, p. 14; © CORBIS, p. 15; Picture History/Newscom, p. 16; The Granger Collection, New York, p. 17; © MPI/Stringer/Archive Photos/Getty Images, pp. 18–19; © American Antiquarian Society, Worcester, Massachusetts, USA/The Bridgeman Art Library, p. 20; Library of Congress rbpe 0370300c, p. 22; © Philadelphia History Museum at the Atwater Kent/Courtesy of Historical Society of Pennsylvania Collection/The Bridgeman Art Library, pp. 23, 28; © Guildhall Art Gallery, City of London/The Bridgeman Art Library, p. 24; © National Geographic Creative/The Bridgeman Art Library, p. 25; © Archive Photos /Getty Images, p. 26; Gift of Mr. and Mrs. George W. Davison/image courtesy of the Board of Trustees, National Gallery of Art, Washington, DC, p. 29; © Museum of Fine Arts, Boston, Massachusetts, USA/Gift of Howland S. Warren/The Bridgeman Art Library, p. 30; © The Huntington Library, Art Collections & Botanical Gardens/The Bridgeman Art Library, p. 32; © Private Collection/Photo © Christie's Images/The Bridgeman Art Library, p. 33; © Stock Montage/Archive Photos/Getty Images, p. 34; U.S. Diplomacy Center /Wikimedia Commons, p. 36; National Archives, p. 37; © Metropolitan Museum of Art, New York, USA/The Bridgeman Art Library, p. 38; Superstock/Courtesy Everett Collection, p. 40; © Kean Collection/Archive Photos/Getty Images, pp. 41, 42; © Jonathan Ernst/Reuters/CORBIS, p. 43.

Front Cover: Architect of the Capitol.

Main text font set in Caecilia Com 55 Rom 11/16.
Typeface provided by Linotype AG.